Wuthering Heights

Emily Brontë
Retold by Peter Viney

---

wuthering Yorkshire pronunciation of 'withering'. A withering look is a look that makes someone feel silly or ashamed

withered something that is withered has become smaller, often older and drier

withering heat or wind that is withering is extremely strong and drying

heights a high place in the country; the top of a hill

Garnet
Oracle

Garnet
EDUCATION

Peter Viney – Series Editor of the Garnet Oracle Readers – has over 40 years' experience teaching English and writing ELT materials. He now combines his writing with lecturing and teacher-training commitments internationally. He has authored and co-authored many successful textbook series and developed a wide range of highly popular video courses. Peter has been series editor and author on a number of graded reader series, and has also published with Garnet Education the highly popular *Fast Track to Reading*.

Published by
Garnet Publishing Ltd.
8 Southern Court
South Street
Reading RG1 4QS, UK

www.garneteducation.com

Copyright © Garnet Publishing Ltd 2014

The right of Peter Viney to be identified as the author of this work has been asserted in accordance with the Copyright, Design and Patents Act 1988.

978-1-78260-229-3

British Cataloguing-in-Publication Data
A catalogue record for this book is available from the British Library.

Production

Series editor:	Peter Viney
Project manager:	Clare Chandler
Editorial:	Lucy Constable
Design and layout:	Mike Hinks
Illustration:	Classical Comics
Cover image:	Getty Images
Photography:	Shutterstock

Printed and bound in Lebanon by
International Press: interpress@int-press.com

2

Emily Brontë

Emily Brontë was born in 1818, and died at the age of thirty in 1848. She was one of the three 'Brontë Sisters' who all wrote novels. Charlotte Brontë wrote *Jane Eyre* and Ann Brontë wrote *Agnes Grey*. They were all published in the same year, 1847. Two of the novels, *Wuthering Heights* and *Jane Eyre*, are among the very best novels in English. They're also two of the most popular. The sisters all came from the same cold Yorkshire house. They were published with men's names because they thought people would not read a book by a woman. Emily was 'Ellis Bell'. Emily died in 1848, and Charlotte published a new edition of *Wuthering Heights* in 1850 with Emily's real name on it. There have been four major films and several TV series of the story.

The Earnshaws

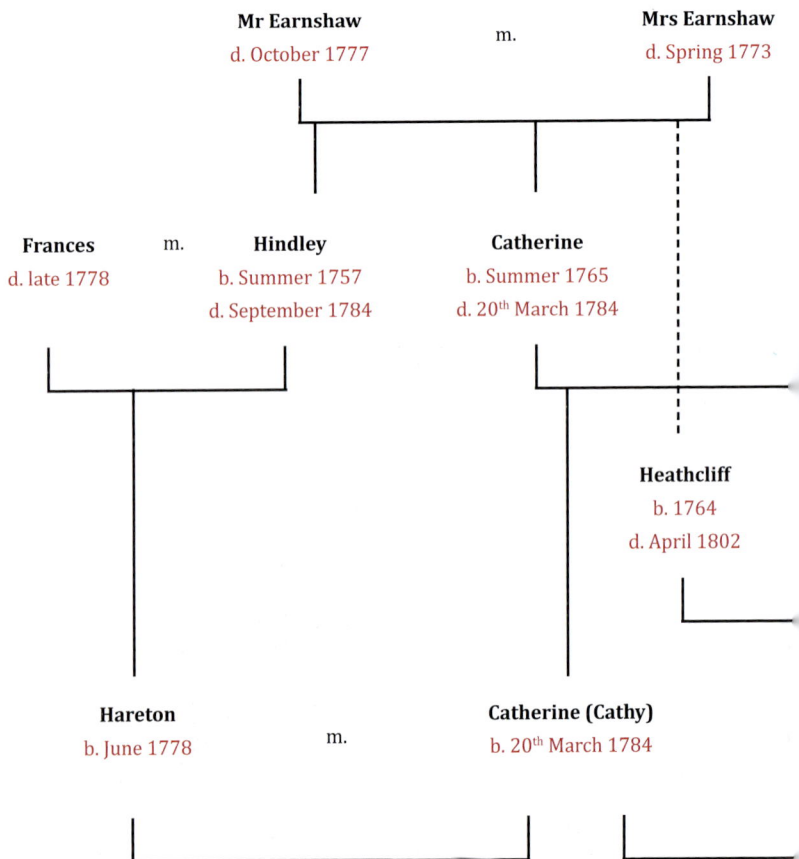

Mr Earnshaw
d. October 1777

m.

Mrs Earnshaw
d. Spring 1773

Frances
d. late 1778

m.

Hindley
b. Summer 1757
d. September 1784

Catherine
b. Summer 1765
d. 20th March 1784

Heathcliff
b. 1764
d. April 1802

Hareton
b. June 1778

m.

Catherine (Cathy)
b. 20th March 1784

and The Lintons

Mr Linton
d. Autumn 1780

m.

Mrs Linton
d. Autumn 1780

m.

Edgar
b. 1762
d. August 1801

m.

Isabella
b. late 1765
d. July 1797

m.

Linton
b. September 1784
d. September 1801

b. = **born**

d. = **died**

m. = **married**

1 My first visit

1801 – Mr Lockwood arrives …

This is a beautiful part of England!

Mr Lockwood's story: November 1801

I shall tell you about my first visit to my landlord, who is my only neighbour here on the lonely Yorkshire moors. It is beautiful country, but it is wild and empty. I rode my horse to his home, Wuthering Heights, which is an old stone building. The walls are thick and strong; the windows are narrow. You can see the power of the cold north wind around the house. The few trees are small, withered and bending away from the wind.

My landlord came out when he heard my horse.

'Mr Heathcliff?' I enquired.

He nodded, without speaking.

'I am Mr Lockwood, and I have just rented your other house, The Grange, and so I thought that I should …'

'Walk in,' he grunted.

'Thank you, sir,' I replied.

'Joseph,' he shouted. 'Take Mr Lockwood's horse to the stable.'

Joseph appeared from the house. He was an old man, no, a very old man, and bent and twisted, though he looked strong. I looked above the door and saw the name HARETON EARNSHAW 1500 cut into the stone. The front door opened straight into the large living room, with no hall or corridor. A huge fire of wood was burning. I could see guns on the stone wall above it. It was like many old Yorkshire farmhouses.

Mr Heathcliff was a tall, handsome man, wearing the clothes of a country gentleman. His eyes were dark, his hair was black, and he looked more like a gypsy than a blond Yorkshire man. His face was sad.

'Where's Joseph gone?' he said, and walked into a back room to find the servant.

Then I saw the three dogs, standing in the dark corner, staring at me. I put out a hand to touch the nearest animal, and it jumped straight at my face. I pushed it back, and then all three dogs were snarling at me. I shouted for help, and my landlord ran into the room and beat them away from me with his stick.

'Those dogs are dangerous, sir …' I started to say.

'We rarely have guests here. And we need guard dogs,' he said, without apologizing. 'Sit down …'

I spent an hour talking to him, mostly about The Grange – the house I was renting. I found him intelligent and interesting. However, I wondered why he was renting The Grange to me. It was a far better house than Wuthering Heights. I asked if I might visit him the next day to talk more. He did not seem pleased, but I decided to call on him anyway.

2 A dark and stormy night

The next afternoon was foggy and cold. It was a good day for sitting by the fire, but I decided to walk the four miles to Wuthering Heights. I arrived just as it began snowing. I knocked hard on the door until Joseph opened it.

'Go away!' he said. 'There's nobody here but the mistress. She won't let you in.'

At that moment a young man walked round the side of the house, carrying a garden fork. In spite of the snow, he was wearing neither coat nor jacket over his shirt.

'Follow me,' he said in a rough voice.

I followed him through a side door into the kitchen, then through to the living room. A young lady was sitting by the fire. I smiled and waited, but she did not offer me a seat.

'Terrible weather,' I said.

She just stared at me. 'You should not have come out,' she said. 'You were not invited.'

'He will be back soon,' said the young man. 'Sit there.'

The young man threw himself back into a chair, and put his feet, still in dirty boots, on a small table. We all sat in silence until Heathcliff returned. Snow was lying thick on his coat.

'Good evening, sir,' I said. 'May I stay for an hour? The snow is falling so heavily.'

'Are you mad?' he said. 'People get lost on these moors in the snow and die. The weather will get worse too.'

I was nervous. 'I am happy to meet your wife, Mrs Heathcliff,' I said.

'My wife is dead. This is my daughter-in-law.'

Heathcliff was about forty. I could see now that the lady was only about seventeen. Obviously she was married to the very rude young man.

'You're a lucky man,' I turned to him, 'to have such a lovely wife.'

His face went red. He looked angry.

'You are wrong again,' said Heathcliff. 'Her husband is dead. She is my daughter-in-law, so she must have married my son.'

'So this young man is ...'

'This young man is not my son,' said Heathcliff.

'I am Hareton Earnshaw,' said the young man, 'and I advise you to respect my name.'

There was silence again. I heard the wind outside. I looked at the window. 'I don't think I can possibly walk home tonight,' I said. 'May I stay here?'

'We have no rooms for guests,' said Heathcliff.

'Perhaps I can sleep in this chair,' I suggested.

'No, I do not want strangers walking around the house at night. You must share a bed with Joseph or Hareton. Or walk across the moor.' He turned and called, 'Zilla!'

An old woman servant appeared.

'Take him into the kitchen,' he ordered. 'Give him some soup.'

3 The face at the window

The house was dark and quiet. Zilla gave me a candle and told me to follow her. 'Do not make any noise,' she said.

We climbed the stairs and walked along a dark corridor. 'My master never lets anyone use this room, but it is empty,' she whispered. 'I do not know why. I have only lived here for two years.'

She left me and closed the door. The bed was in a kind of cupboard, something you find in houses of two or three hundred years ago. I opened the doors, and found the bed, which was covered with thick dust. It was next to the window, with a wooden shelf under the window, on which were a few old books. I put the candle on the shelf. Names were cut into the wood. I moved away some dust and read them. CATHERINE EARNSHAW, CATHERINE LINTON and CATHERINE HEATHCLIFF. The names were repeated many times. I picked up a book, and opened it. *Catherine Earnshaw* was written on the first page in a child's writing.

I looked at the books, but I was tired and soon fell asleep, dreaming of walking through deep snow.

I woke suddenly to the sound of the wind and the tapping of a tree branch against the window. I tried to open the window, but it was locked. The tap-tap-tap of the branch continued. How could I stop it? I knocked my hand hard on one of the small squares of glass and it broke. I put my arm through to reach the branch, and then my fingers closed on the fingers of a little ice-cold hand.

I thought I was still dreaming. I tried to pull my arm back, but the hand would not let go of mine.

'Let me in … Let me in,' cried a small sad voice.

'Who are you?' I asked.

'Catherine Linton. I've come home. I lost my way on the moor.'

As the voice spoke, I saw a girl's face looking through the window, tiny and white.

'Let me go!' I cried. I pulled my hand back, but the little white hand stayed holding mine, and was cut on the broken glass. Blood ran down the glass onto the shelf. The fingers finally let go of mine.

'Twenty years!' said the sad little voice. 'Twenty years. I've been alone for almost twenty years.'

I screamed in fright and jumped away from the window.

I heard my door open and the sound of feet. 'Is anyone in here?' It was Heathcliff.

'It is only me, sir. Mr Lockwood ...' I replied. 'I had a terrible, terrible dream! I woke up. A girl ... Catherine Linton or Earnshaw or whatever she was called ... She was trying to get in the window ... Look at the blood!'

But there was no blood on the window or the shelf.

'This room is haunted!' I cried. 'She must be a ghost!'

'You left this candle by this window?' shouted Heathcliff. 'By this window!' He climbed quickly onto the bed by the window. 'Cathy!' he called. 'Cathy! Come in! Do come in! Hear me this time, my darling!'

I hurried downstairs, and walked around the kitchen until the first light of morning. Then I walked home to The Grange, across the moor, falling up to my neck in deep snow several times. My servants ran out to meet me, and soon I had a hot bath, warm clothes and a hot coffee in my hand.

4 Nellie's story begins

I was now curious about Wuthering Heights. The housekeeper at The Grange, Mrs Dean, was employed by Heathcliff. So when she brought my dinner to the table, I asked, 'Have you lived here for a long time, Mrs Dean?'

'I came to The Grange eighteen years ago, sir, when my late mistress was married. After she died, the master kept me here as the housekeeper.'

'You must have seen many changes,' I said.

'I have, sir. And many troubles too.'

'I wonder, Mrs Dean, why Mr Heathcliff rents out The Grange when it so much larger and more pleasing than Wuthering Heights. Is it too expensive for him?'

'Why, sir,' she said, 'he will be the richest man you know. And every year he gets richer.'

'He had a son, I believe.'

'Yes, sir. He had one. He is dead.'

'And the young lady, Mrs Heathcliff, is the son's widow?'

'She is, sir. She is my poor late mistress's daughter. Catherine Linton was her name before she was married. I was her nurse, sir. I looked after her from her first day in this world. I only wish I could be with her again.'

'Catherine Linton?' I said. I felt cold ice at the back of my neck. 'Then her mother's name was Linton?'

'It was after she married. But her mother was an Earnshaw. Her name used to be Catherine Earnshaw …'

Another name from my dream, but that part was not a dream. The name was in the book.

Mrs Dean continued. '... and Catherine Earnshaw lived at Wuthering Heights, until she married Edgar Linton from The Grange, and so then she became Catherine Linton too.'

Earnshaw. The name cut in the stone over the door to Wuthering Heights. 'Who is the young man, Hareton Earnshaw, who lives with Mr Heathcliff?'

'My late mistress was his aunt, sir. He is her brother's son.'

'So he is the young lady's cousin, then.'

'Yes, sir. Her late husband was her cousin, too. Mr Heathcliff married Mr Edgar Linton's sister.'

I shook my head. 'This is all very difficult to understand, Mrs Dean. What can you tell me about Mr Heathcliff?'

'Everything, sir. Except where he was born, who his parents were and how he got his money. I know nothing of that.' She smiled. 'It's a long story, sir.'

I pointed to the chair beside the fire. 'Then please sit down and join me, Mrs Dean. I should like to hear it ...'

Understanding the Story 1 (Chapters 1–4)

1 Look at these sentences about the people in the story. Match the two parts. All the sentences must match once.

1	Heathcliff was …	A	… Heathcliff's daughter-in-law.
2	Joseph was …	B	… the man who had rented The Grange from Heathcliff.
3	The young woman was …	C	… a ghost.
4	Hareton Earnshaw was …	D	… Mr Lockwood's landlord.
5	Mr Lockwood was …	E	… the housekeeper at The Grange.
6	Zilla was …	F	… an old servant who took the horse to the stable.
7	The voice at the window was …	G	… the servant who showed Lockwood to his room.
8	Mrs Dean was…	H	… not Heathcliff's son.

2 Number the things Mr Lockwood did in order from 1 (earliest in the story) to 10 (latest in the story).

_____ He heard a girl's voice outside the window.

_____ He spent an hour talking to Heathcliff.

_____ He told Heathcliff he had had a terrible dream.

_____ He asked if he might stay for the night.

_____ He met Hareton and Heathcliff's daughter-in-law.

_____ He rode to Wuthering Heights.

_____ He saw three names cut into the wood by the window.

_____ He hurried to the kitchen and spent the night there.

_____ He asked Mrs Dean to tell him about Heathcliff.

_____ He walked the four miles to Wuthering Heights.

3 **Look at the names in Activity 1. Heathcliff is number 1, Joseph is number 2, the young woman is number 3, etc. Who said these things? (Some spoke more than once). Put the numbers next to the sentences.**

_____ 'We rarely have guests here. And we need guard dogs.'

_____ 'There's nobody here but the mistress. She won't let you in.'

_____ 'You should not have come out. You were not invited.'

_____ 'May I stay for an hour? The snow is falling so heavily.'

_____ 'And I advise you to respect my name.'

_____ 'You must share a bed with Joseph or Hareton.'

_____ 'Do not make any noise.'

_____ 'I've come home. I lost my way on the moor.'

_____ 'This room is haunted! She must be a ghost.'

_____ 'You must have seen many changes.'

_____ 'Everything, sir. Except where he was born, who his parents were and how he got his money.'

5 The early days

Nellie Dean's story: 1771 to 1777

I used to work at Wuthering Heights, just as my mother did before me. The Earnshaws were farmers, not rich people like their neighbours at The Grange, the Lintons. There were only two servants then, me and Joseph, whom you have met.

Mr and Mrs Earnshaw had two children. Hindley was fourteen when my story begins, and Cathy, or Catherine, was just six. She was a wild child, always laughing, always asking questions, always joking, never sitting still.

Old Mr Earnshaw had travelled to Liverpool on some business, and the children were waiting for his return. He walked in one evening, wearing a great coat, which he opened to reveal a small boy. He had found the child in the streets of Liverpool, alone and hungry. We came close to look. The boy was about Cathy's age. His clothes were rags. He was dirty from head to foot, and he had black, curly hair and black eyes.

'He looks like a gypsy!' said Mrs Earnshaw, and called to me. 'Nellie,' she said. 'Take him to the kitchen, throw away those dirty rags and wash him with soap and hot water!'

I took the boy's hand, and he started speaking, but we could not understand a word.

'What shall we do with him?' cried Mrs Earnshaw. 'Because he cannot stay here!'

'There is nowhere else,' said Mr Earnshaw. 'He will stay here and live with us, and we shall call him Heathcliff.'

And that became his name. It was his first name and his family name. He had no other.

Miss Cathy and Heathcliff soon became the best of friends. They were always together. But Hindley was jealous, and hated him. He would bully him. He would push him, hit him and beat him every day. Heathcliff was much younger and smaller, but he never cried out, or ran away from Hindley. He just stared. He soon learned to speak, and the three children had lessons together from a teacher who visited the house.

Old Mr Earnshaw was angry about this bullying. He seemed to like Heathcliff best of all the children, more even than Cathy. This made Hindley's jealousy worse.

I remember one day. Mr Earnshaw had bought horses for each of the children. The three children were out riding, and Heathcliff's horse was injured, and could only walk slowly with pain back to the stable.

Heathcliff went to Hindley and said, 'You must change horses with me. I don't like mine. If you won't change, I shall tell your father about the three beatings yesterday. I'll show him my arm, which is black to the shoulder from your beatings.'

Hindley pushed him to the ground.

'You must do it,' said Heathcliff, getting up, 'because if I speak about the beatings you gave me, your father will beat you.'

At this, Hindley picked up a large stone.

'Throw it,' said Heathcliff, 'and I will tell your father of your words yesterday. You said you would throw me out of the house as soon as he was dead.'

Hindley threw the stone straight at Heathcliff's head. He fell to the ground again. Cathy ran to him crying. 'You have killed him!' Hindley just laughed and walked away. Then Heathcliff stood up calmly, his head bleeding. I ran over to help him. He looked at me. He did not cry, though blood was running down his shirt. Hindley's anger was always hot and quick. Heathcliff's anger was more frightening, because it was slow and cold, even when he was young.

Mrs Earnshaw died less than two years after Heathcliff arrived. Mr Earnshaw was not in good health himself after his wife's death, and the fighting between the children tired him. After a time, Hindley was sent away to college. Then there was peace in the house. Cathy and Heathcliff were left free to ride over the moors, or to climb the tall rocks on the hill near the house. Heathcliff used to call the rocks their 'castle'. They were like wild children, only happy in each other's company.

One night Mr Earnshaw was asleep in the chair, or so I thought. Joseph went to wake him and stopped. He spoke to the children, who were playing a game in front of the fire. Joseph's voice was strange and different. 'You children! Go to bed now … Go on! Go when I tell you!'

Cathy never listened to instructions. 'I'll kiss father goodnight first!' she said, and ran over to the poor man's chair, and put her arms around his neck. She froze. 'He's dead!' she screamed. 'Father is dead.'

Later that night, after the doctor had left, I went up to Cathy's room. The two children were there together, lying on the floor, and talking so sweetly about the poor late master.

6 The Lintons

Hindley came back home for the funeral, and there was a surprise. He brought his new wife with him. Her name was Frances, but he told us nothing about her. Not where she was born, nor who her family was. Frances was young, and she told Cathy she was happy to have a sister-in-law. I should have noticed she was ill that first night. She was thin, and her eyes were always very bright. She found the stairs difficult, and breathed heavily when she was climbing them. She stopped at the top and coughed for two minutes. But I had other things to worry about.

First, Hindley told Joseph and me to move from the house to the outside farm building. He wanted the house for himself, not for servants. Then he told Heathcliff to join us and take the room above the stable. From then on, Heathcliff would work on the farm as another servant. He would have no more lessons with Miss Cathy.

Hindley was not interested in the younger children. They ran wild over the moors, and very often Heathcliff was beaten by Hindley, who seemed to enjoy bullying him.

One night, the children annoyed him, and he locked them in a room. I went to call the children for dinner, and when I opened the door, they were not there. The window was open, and they had gone. Hindley told us to lock all the doors and said they could stay out all night.

It was freezing cold and raining heavily. I waited until the master was asleep, and opened the front door. I watched the dark moor for a long time, and then I heard feet. It was Heathcliff. And he was alone.

'Where is Miss Catherine?' I cried in fear. 'Has there been an accident?'

'She's at The Grange,' he said, 'with the Lintons. I should have stayed with her, but they would not allow me.'

Heathcliff told me the story. 'We escaped through the window, Nellie,' he started. 'We were on the moor, and we saw the lights from the Linton's house. We thought it would be funny to look closer, so we climbed the wall, and went quietly up to the window. We looked through and saw Edgar Linton and his sister, Isabella. They were quarrelling over a silly game. Both of them were crying like babies! We laughed loudly, and they turned and saw our faces through the window. They screamed for their father. We started running away, but he let the guard dogs out, and they chased us. One dog caught Cathy and savagely bit her

Run, Heathcliff!

the ankle. I turned and pulled the dog away. I was trying to kill
with my hands, because Cathy was hurt, and her ankle was
eeding badly. But then Mr Linton and his servants arrived. They
ught us both. They thought we were robbers.'

aw that Heathcliff's hand was hurt, where the dog had bitten
m too. He continued. 'Mr Linton carried Cathy indoors. They
lled me in too. When they got into the light, they recognized
thy. They knew who I was, but they threw me out of the house.
'hrow that little gypsy out!" said Mr Linton. They told me she
ould stay there until her ankle was better. I went back and
atched through the window. She is still there.'

7 A fine young lady

Cathy stayed with the Lintons at The Grange for five weeks. The mistress, Frances, used to visit her. When Cathy returned to Wuthering Heights, she looked like a different person. Her hair was carefully arranged in curls, and her dress was beautiful and expensive. She was wearing a fine hat.

'Nellie,' the mistress said to me. 'Help Miss Catherine with her hat. We must be careful with her lovely curls.'

Hindley said, 'You look like a fine lady now, Catherine. We must not let you run wild again.'

'Where is Heathcliff?' asked Cathy.

Heathcliff was in the kitchen, watching from the door.

'Heathcliff,' said Hindley. 'You may come forward and welcome Miss Catherine, like the other servants.'

Cathy ran to him. 'Heathcliff! How angry and dirty you look! I expect that's because Edgar and Isabella Linton are always clean, and they are always smiling! Have you forgotten me?'

'I shall not stand here while you laugh at me,' said Heathcliff.

'But you look so funny!' she said. 'Why don't you wash your face and brush your hair?'

'I like to be dirty, and I shall be dirty,' said Heathcliff, and walked out of the room.

After that though, Heathcliff washed carefully, and he asked me to cut his hair. He was jealous of Edgar Linton and unhappy that Cathy spoke about Edgar all the time.

'I'm nobody, Nellie,' he said. 'I may be stronger than Edgar, but he is rich, and I never shall be. Nobody knows who I am.'

'Heathcliff,' I said. 'We don't know who your parents were. Maybe your father was the Emperor of China and your mother was an Indian queen. If I were you, I would think about that and feel better about myself.'

The Lintons came to visit us. Heathcliff walked into the room where everyone was sitting. His hair was cut, and I had washed his shirt and trousers.

Hindley laughed. 'Get back out to the stable, Heathcliff. This is not a place for servants.'

Edgar laughed too. 'He is a stupid farm boy,' he said. 'Does he think he is a gentleman?'

In a moment, Heathcliff had picked up a large bowl of hot apple sauce from the table and emptied it over Edgar's head.

Hindley pulled Heathcliff outside to the room over the stable and beat him for a long time. Then he locked the door, and ordered that no one should give him any food.

Later that night, I took a bowl of soup and went quietly to Heathcliff's room. To my surprise, I heard voices inside. Cathy had climbed onto the stable roof and climbed through the roof window over Heathcliff's prison. They were sitting there, eating food that Cathy had brought from the kitchen.

I sat with them. Heathcliff was staring at the wall.

'What are you thinking of, Heathcliff?' I asked.

'One day I shall pay Hindley back, Nellie,' he said coldly. 'One day I will have my revenge. It may take many years, but I will do it. I hope that he will not die before I do.'

8 Anger

On the morning of a fine June day in 1778, the last child with the Earnshaw name was born. They named the child Hareton – the name which is cut in stone over the door. The doctor told me that the new mother, my mistress, Frances, was very ill and would be dead by winter. Hindley would not believe that she was ill, and every day said that he thought she was getting better. But she never left her bed again. One night she told Hindley that she hoped to get up the next day. Then she coughed badly. Hindley took her in his arms to help her, but in a second she was dead.

Hindley did not cry. He became more cruel and wicked. He attacked Heathcliff every day, kicking and beating him. I wanted to go away from that house, but I could not leave little Hareton there. I was his nurse, and I had to protect him. Hindley's only interest was gambling and playing cards with some of the worst men from the moors. He would sit all night, cards in his hand, throwing money onto the table. Heathcliff used to watch him, with a strange smile on his face.

One day, when Miss Cathy was sixteen, I was cleaning the room when Mr Edgar Linton arrived. Little Hareton was sitting on the floor next to me. Cathy was wearing her best blue dress. She called to me, 'Nellie, we have a guest. Stop cleaning and go somewhere else. Servants should not clean when guests are visiting.'

'I'm sure Mr Linton will excuse me,' I said. 'I have to finish my work.'

Cathy was standing by me. She took my arm between her fingers and pinched me hard. 'Now go!' she whispered.

'Ow!' I shouted in pain. 'You may be my mistress, but it is not right for you to pinch me!'

'I did not touch you,' she said. 'You are lying!'

I pointed to the red pinch mark on my arm. 'So what is this?' I said.

'Leave the room immediately!' she shouted.

Little Hareton suddenly spoke. 'Bad Aunt Cathy!' he said. 'Wicked!'

Cathy was so angry. She raised her hand to hit the child. Edgar shouted, 'No!' and put out his hand to stop her. She turned and hit Edgar across the face, as hard as she could.

Edgar walked to the door.

'Stay! You shall not leave!' she said.

'I cannot stay,' he said. 'You have hit me. And you have lied about Nellie and pinched her. I shall never come here again.'

Cathy fell to the floor crying terribly. 'Then I will cry until I am sick and I die!' she said.

Edgar stopped, waited, and then ran back to help her to her feet. 'I am so sorry, Cathy ... So sorry ...' he was saying.

I watched him. 'Ah,' I thought to myself. 'There will be no saving that young man. Like a fish on a line, he is caught! He will not escape her.'

It was the day after Catherine and Edgar's quarrel. Hindley arrived home after gambling all night and all day. For weeks, Hindley used to forget about his son, but the child was happy with me, or with Cathy. Then Hindley would become angry because Hareton was frightened of him. I was cleaning upstairs. He saw the boy with me and said, 'Come and greet your father, Hareton!'

But Hareton held onto my skirt in fear. 'No!' he said.

Hindley climbed the stairs. 'Kiss your father, boy!' he shouted. He picked the boy up in his arms.

'No!' screamed the boy, kicking his father.

'I'll break the child's neck!' shouted Hindley angrily.

At that moment we heard the sound of feet downstairs. Hindley looked down, forgetting about the child kicking and trying to escape from his arms. Then Hareton was out of his father's arms and falling …

And the child was saved! We saw that he had fallen straight into Heathcliff's arms, because it was Heathcliff who was walking through the hall. Heathcliff had caught him automatically, without thinking. I saw Heathcliff's face. I could see how sorry he was to catch the child. He had stopped his own revenge on the child's father.

I ran down to take the terrified boy. His father walked slowly downstairs.

'This is your fault, Nellie,' he said. 'You should have taken the boy from me. Is he injured?'

'Injured?' I cried angrily. 'He would have been killed if Heathcliff had not saved him!'

'Heathcliff? Yes, get out of the house, Heathcliff,' he snarled. 'Go and do your work in the stable!'

Understanding the Story 2
(Chapters 5–8)

1 **Look at these sentences about the people in the story. Match the two halves to make sentences. All the sentences must match once.**

1	Old Mr Earnshaw ...	A	... owned The Grange.
2	Cathy ...	B	... was a bully.
3	Hindley ...	C	... called Heathcliff 'a stupid farm boy.'
4	Frances ...	D	... was Edgar's sister.
5	Mr Linton ...	E	... found the boy in Liverpool.
6	Edgar Linton ...	F	... was born in 1778.
7	Hareton ...	G	... was the same age as the boy.
8	Isabella ...	H	... married Cathy's older brother.

2 **Match the descriptions. Write the name of the character next to the descriptions.**

1 _____ His clothes were rags. He was dirty from head to foot, and he had black, curly hair and black eyes.

2 _____ He was a bully. He was jealous. His anger was always hot and quick.

3 _____ She was a wild child, always laughing, always asking questions, always joking, never sitting still.

4 _____ She was young. She was thin and weak. Her eyes were always bright. She had a terrible cough.

5 _____ He was a rich man with a large house and several servants. He had a son and a daughter.

6 _____ He was always clean and well-dressed. He had rich parents. He was rude to Heathcliff.

7 _____ His mother died soon after he was born. He was afraid of his father.

8 _____ She was a servant. One of her jobs was to look after the baby after his mother had died.

3 Number these events in order from 1 (earliest in the story) to 10 (latest in the story).

_____ Hindley threw a stone at Heathcliff.

_____ Hindley came home for the funeral with a wife.

_____ Heathcliff poured hot apple sauce over Edgar.

_____ Cathy and Heathcliff soon became the best of friends.

_____ A dog caught Cathy and bit her ankle.

_____ Hindley began gambling with bad men.

_____ Mr Earnshaw died in his chair.

_____ Heathcliff caught Hareton in his arms and saved his life.

_____ Cathy stayed with the Lintons at The Grange for five weeks.

_____ Heathcliff and Cathy escaped from a window.

9 Talk of marriage

I took the frightened Hareton into the kitchen, and held the boy until he fell asleep in my arms.

Cathy came into the kitchen. 'Are you alone, Nellie?' she asked.

'Yes, Miss. Heathcliff's working with the horses in the stable.'

'Can you keep a secret for me, Nellie?' she said. 'Today Edgar Linton has asked me to marry him. I have given him my answer. Before I tell you what my answer was, you can tell me what it ought to have been.'

'How do I know, Miss Catherine,' I said. 'After yesterday's quarrel, he must be a fool.'

'I said "yes" to him, Nellie. Was I right or was I wrong?'

'You have given your promise now, Miss. You cannot change that. Do you love him?'

'Of course I do.'

'Why do you love him, Miss Cathy?'

'Nonsense! I do. That's all.'

'You must tell me why.'

'Because he's handsome and good to be with.'

'Bad reasons,' I said.

'Because he's young, and always happy.'

'Bad again.'

'And because he loves me.'

'Neither good nor bad,' I said.

'And because he will be rich. I shall be the richest woman on the Yorkshire Moors. And I shall be proud of having Edgar as my husband.'

'That's the worst reason of all,' I said, 'but if you love him and have agreed to marry him, then what is the problem?'

Cathy put her hand to her head, then to her heart. 'Because here in my head and here in my heart, whichever place my soul lives in, I am sure that I am wrong!'

She put her head against the wall and murmured softly, 'If that wicked man, my brother, had not brought Heathcliff so low, I would never have thought of marrying Edgar.'

I thought I heard someone moving in the kitchen.

Cathy continued, more loudly. 'But it would degrade me to marry Heathcliff now! It would bring me down to his low position in life! Heathcliff will never know how much I love him. He is more myself than I am! I don't know what souls are, but his and mine are the same! My soul and Edgar's soul are as different as fire and ice!'

While she was talking, I had turned my head a little. I could not move more because of the child in my arms. I saw Heathcliff rise from a chair and go quietly out of the kitchen door. He had stayed long enough to hear her say that it would degrade her to marry him, but he had not heard the rest of her words! Then I heard another door opening.

'Shh …' I said. 'I can hear Joseph coming, and Heathcliff will probably be with him.'

'Give me Hareton,' she said. 'I'll hold him for you while you prepare dinner.'

Joseph walked in.

'Is Heathcliff with you?' I asked.

'No,' he growled. 'Isn't he in here?'

'No,' I said. 'I'll go and call him for dinner. I expect he's in the stable.'

I went out and called, but there was no answer. When I returned, I whispered to Cathy. I told her that Heathcliff must have heard her. I said that he had left the kitchen after she had said it would degrade her to marry him.

Cathy ran outside to the front of the house, calling 'Heathcliff!' She would not come back in, but stayed out there, looking out across the moor, even though it started raining. Then thunder crashed and lightning flashed across the dark sky. At midnight, I brought her indoors.

'He will not be back tonight,' I said. 'He will be in the village. He must have stayed there in Gimmerton. You cannot wait any longer.'

She would not go to bed, but sat in her wet dress next to the fire. She was still there the next morning. Hindley sent her to her room. He was more angry with her than worried about her. When I got her to the bedroom, she began screaming and crying. I thought she was going mad! She would not eat nor drink. At last, Hindley agreed to send for the doctor. He said she was dangerously ill. Her head and body were hot, and she muttered words we could not understand.

She was sick for many weeks.

10 Leaving home

Catherine survived. When she started to feel better, old Mrs Linton invited her to stay at The Grange. I have to say we were pleased to have a rest from her bad temper. While she was at The Grange, Mrs Linton and Mr Linton both became sick, and they died within a few days of each other.

So our young lady returned to Wuthering Heights, grander and ruder to us servants than ever before. Heathcliff had never been heard of since the evening of the thunderstorm. One day, when Cathy had been ordering me around for hours, I said that Heathcliff disappearing was her fault. It was true, but she did not forgive me for months. The doctor told us that we must not make her angry, or put her in a bad temper, or her illness might return. Even Hindley was careful, and he wanted her to marry Edgar Linton.

Three years later, Edgar and Catherine were married in Gimmerton, and Edgar told us that he was now the happiest man in the world. Catherine asked me to move to The Grange with her, but I refused. Hareton was only five years old and I was teaching him to read and write.

When I refused she complained first to her husband, and he offered me more money than I was earning at Wuthering Heights. I refused again, so she complained to her brother, who ordered me out of Wuthering Heights. He said that now Cathy had gone, he had no work for women servants. Joseph was the only servant he needed.

I was very sad when I kissed Hareton goodbye. Since that day he has been a stranger to me, and I'm afraid he has forgotten all about Nellie Dean. For his first five years, he meant more than the whole world to me and me to him. Then I started my new life at The Grange.

Cathy behaved better than I had expected in her new home. The house was much larger and brighter than Wuthering Heights, with large windows and beautiful furniture. I began to know Edgar, and found that he was a kind and good man. Cathy seemed happy. She seemed to love Edgar very much, and Edgar and Isabella were both kind and affectionate to her.

One September evening, I was in the garden picking apples from the trees. I heard a voice from the bushes. 'Nellie! Is that you?'

'Who is it?'

'Don't you know me? I have been waiting here for an hour. Look, I am not a stranger …'

The man came out from the bushes. He was wearing the expensive clothes of a gentleman. I was so shocked that I dropped my basket of apples.

'Heathcliff!' I said. 'Is it really you?'

He helped me to pick up the apples. 'Is she here?' he said. 'I must have a few words with your mistress. Go and tell her someone from Gimmerton wants to see her.'

'I dare not! The shock will make her mad!'

'Go!' he said. 'Do not dare to refuse me!'

Edgar and Cathy were in the sitting room.

'A person from Gimmerton wishes to see you, ma'am,' I said. 'He is at the front door.'

Cathy left the room.

'Who is it, Nellie?' said Edgar.

'A visitor we did not expect, sir,' I said. 'It is Heathcliff, who used to live at Wuthering Heights.'

'The gypsy farm boy?' said Edgar. 'Why didn't you tell us?'

Catherine came back into the room. 'Oh, Edgar! Darling! Heathcliff has come back!' She put her arms around Edgar.

'I know you didn't like him. But you must be friends now! Nellie, tell him to come into the sitting room.'

'Here? Into our sitting room? Catherine! Don't be silly!' said Edgar. 'You cannot welcome a servant who ran away like a brother!'

I brought Heathcliff into the room. Cathy took his arm, led him to Mr Linton and made them shake hands. I was amazed at how different Heathcliff looked. He was taller than Edgar now, and looked quiet but powerful. Only three years had passed, but his face looked much older, and he was polite and spoke well. He stood straight like a soldier, or a fine gentleman.

Edgar wasn't sure how to speak to him. 'Sit down, sir,' he said politely. 'Mrs Linton remembers you well and wishes me to welcome you to our home. And I am happy to do anything which pleases her.'

'I shall stay an hour or two then,' said Heathcliff.

Catherine spoke. 'I shall think this is a dream tomorrow. But Heathcliff, you have been away for three years. And you have never thought of me.'

'I have thought of you more than you have thought of me,' he said. 'I heard of your marriage recently, Cathy. While waiting in the garden, I had an idea. I wanted to see your face, just once, then have my revenge on Hindley, and then kill myself. But your welcome has changed my mind. I have had a difficult life since I last heard your voice. You must forgive me, for I have worked only for you.'

There was a long and embarrassing silence. Edgar spoke first. 'Come to the table. Our tea is getting cold. Please ask Isabella to join us, Nellie.'

I left the room. The meal only lasted ten minutes. Neither Heathcliff nor Cathy ate or drank. Heathcliff left after an hour, and I took him to the door.

'Are you staying in Gimmerton, Heathcliff?' I asked.

'No, Wuthering Heights,' he replied. 'Mr Earnshaw invited me when I called this morning.'

I closed the door behind him. He had said *Mr Earnshaw?* And Mr Earnshaw invited *him?* And *he* called on Mr Earnshaw? What were Heathcliff's plans? I should have known that they were wicked ones.

11 Isabella

Cathy was more affectionate to Edgar than ever before. So he did not complain when she visited Wuthering Heights the next day, taking her sister-in-law, Isabella, with her. Heathcliff – I should say Mr Heathcliff in future – was careful about visiting The Grange at first. Then slowly, he began to visit more often.

Mr Linton had new worries, though. His sister, Isabella, was showing signs of affection for Heathcliff. Edgar hated the thought of Isabella falling in love with Heathcliff. First, Heathcliff had no family, no name and no position in life. But he was also worried about The Grange, his land and his money. Until he and Cathy had a son, Isabella was his heir. If he died before having a son, everything he owned would go to Isabella. He did not trust Heathcliff. Heathcliff must know that Isabella was heir to everything.

Cathy and Isabella often quarrelled too. One afternoon, Cathy said, 'Why are you so unhappy, Isabella?'

'You know why! When we were walking across the moor, with Mr Heathcliff, you told me to go and walk somewhere else. You wanted me to go away so you could be alone with him!'

'I hope you did not mean that, Isabella.'

'I did! I love him more than you love Edgar. Mr Heathcliff might love me too, but you will not allow him to!'

Cathy turned to me. 'Nellie! Tell her that she's mad. He is a wild and dangerous person, with no education.'

I was embarrassed, but I said, 'Forget about him, Miss. He is bad luck, believe me. He is no husband for a lady like you.'

The next time Heathcliff visited, I was working in the kitchen by the window. Isabella was walking in the garden. Heathcliff looked up at the house, and I could see that he was checking all the windows. I stepped back, away from the window so that he could not see me. Cathy had come into the kitchen and came to stand next to me, watching. Heathcliff went over to Isabella and kissed her. She pushed him away and hurried to the house.

'He is a wicked cheat!' I said. 'I shall tell the master! He was kissing her!'

Cathy spoke sharply to me. 'Who do you think you are, Nellie? You are speaking like the mistress of the house. Be silent!'

The door opened and Heathcliff came in.

Cathy looked at him. 'I have told you before. You must leave Isabella alone, or the doors to this house will be closed to you.'

'I have every right to kiss Isabella, if she agrees,' said Heathcliff to Cathy. 'And it is none of your business. I am not your husband, so you need not be jealous of me.'

'If you love Isabella, then you may marry her,' said Cathy. 'But do you love her? Tell me the truth.'

'If I really thought you wished me to marry Isabella, I would cut my own throat,' said Heathcliff.

Mr Edgar walked quickly into the room. 'I know what happened,' he said angrily. 'You will leave my house now, and you will never come here again. Go, Heathcliff! You have three minutes to leave!'

Heathcliff laughed in Edgar's face. 'Is your husband a lion or a lamb, Cathy? A lamb, I think.'

Edgar was shaking, with anger or fear or both. Cathy shut the outside door of the house and locked it. She took the key in her hand. 'If you are afraid to attack him, Edgar, then you must apologize to him, or I warn you, he will beat you.'

Edgar tried to take the key from her hand, but she just laughed and threw it into the hottest part of the fire.

'Your husband's a coward, Cathy,' said Heathcliff. 'And you chose him, not me. Look at the lamb, shaking with fear. Is he going to start crying?'

Edgar jumped forward and hit Heathcliff hard in the throat, and then he turned and walked into the hall.

Heathcliff had his hands to his throat, and he was coughing.

'You fool!' said Cathy. 'Now go away! He will return with five or six servants and they'll have guns. Now you will never be able to return here!'

Heathcliff's face was twisted with anger. 'If I do not beat him today, I shall murder him in the future!' he said.

Heathcliff went to the outside door, pulled it hard, and broke the lock with his hands. He walked out.

The master returned with the male servants. They all had weapons.

'So, Catherine,' he said. 'You will stop seeing Heathcliff, or you will stop seeing me. You must choose.'

'We will speak no more of it,' she said. 'Your blood is ice water. And mine is hot fire! Now leave me alone, Edgar!'

She ran to her room and locked the door.

12 A night of fear

Cathy stayed in her room, with the door locked, for three days and nights. Isabella walked sadly up and down the garden. Edgar stayed in the sitting room with his books, reading.

On the third evening, she opened the door to me. She had finished her water, and drank quickly from the glass I gave her.

'Nellie,' she said. 'I will surely die! What has that fool Mr Linton been doing?'

'He has been reading, ma'am.'

'Reading! While I am dying? You are all my enemies here!'

She went to the window and opened it to the freezing air. She stood with her head out in the cold fog, crying and shaking. I tried to get her to bed, but could not move her. Then I went and found the master.

'My mistress is ill, sir. I think she is quite mad. I cannot get her into the bed. Forget your anger, sir, and come and help me with her.'

Edgar came to the room. Her face had changed so much in just a few days. Her face was white. She looked years older.

I was sent to get the doctor immediately, even though it was now late at night. As I passed through the garden, I saw something white, hanging from a tree. I hurried over and found Miss Isabella's little dog, hanging from a rope. The poor animal was nearly dead. I quickly took the rope from its throat, and held it in my arms. What was the dog doing in the garden at night? It always slept under Miss Isabella's bed. I put the dog down. It started running around, smelling the ground. Then I heard something, far away in the night. The sound of horses, and they were moving fast.

I brought the doctor back from the village with me. He said Cathy needed sleep, peace and quiet. The doctor also told us that she was expecting a child, so we had a double reason to look after her.

I sat up beside her bed all night. Mr Linton sat with me and did not close his eyes either. In the morning, all the servants were up early. Edgar was surprised that Isabella was not awake and that she had not asked about poor Cathy. At that moment, Isabella's servant, Mary, ran into the room.

'She's gone, sir! Miss Isabella's gone! Heathcliff has run off with her!'

'This is not true. It cannot be … Why do you say such nonsense?' said Edgar.

Mary told us that she had just met the boy who brought the milk from the farms to the village. He had seen Heathcliff and Isabella on horses during the night, and they were riding away from the moors.

'What should we do, sir?' I asked. 'Shall I send the men to bring her back home?'

Edgar stayed by Cathy's bed. 'She chose to go,' he said. 'I cannot stop her. Tell me no more about her. From this day, she is not my sister.'

We saw nothing of Heathcliff or Isabella. After six weeks, Isabella wrote a letter telling Edgar that she was married to Heathcliff. It was a dry, cold letter, but at the bottom, was an apology, written in pencil.

Edgar looked after Cathy day and night. She could have had no better a nurse than him. By March, her life was no longer in danger. Then I received a letter from Isabella.

Dear Nellie,

We arrived at Wuthering Heights last night, and I heard, for the first time, that Catherine is very ill. I must not write to her, I suppose. And my brother is too angry, or too unhappy, to reply to my letters. I so much wish to see his face again! But I will not be able to visit. You may guess the reason.

Nellie, how did you live at Wuthering Heights? How did you remain a kind, normal person while living here?

Secondly, I must ask you. Is Heathcliff mad? Or is he just a cruel, wicked monster? Please explain to me what I have married. I have been a fool, and I hate him.

You must come and see me soon. Do not write, but visit and bring me some message from Edgar. Do not tell anyone about this letter. I shall wait for you every day.

Isabella

I told the master that his sister had returned. I said she had asked me to visit her, and that she hoped for a message from him.

Edgar looked sad. 'You may call on her at Wuthering Heights. You may go this afternoon, if you like. Say that I am not angry, just sorry because I have lost her. I cannot believe that she will be happy. But I shall never speak to Heathcliff, nor his family.'

13 Heathcliff is back

I walked across the moor the same day, and entered the house without knocking. The house was dark and dirty, with dust everywhere. Heathcliff sat at a table, looking a fine gentleman. But Isabella looked like a servant. She looked tired and ill. Her hair was dirty and her dress was old. She put out her hand, expecting a letter from her brother. I shook my head. Heathcliff saw me. 'Nellie, if you have got anything for Isabella, please give it to her. We have no secrets between us.'

'Oh, I have nothing,' I replied. 'My master says she must not expect either a letter or a visit. He sends his love, but says there can be no contact between his house and yours.'

Heathcliff stood up and began to question me about Cathy. I told him she had been dangerously ill and was still very weak.

'She will never be like she used to be,' I said. 'And if you care about her, you will never contact her again. Another fight between you and the master would kill her.'

'I did not hit Linton,' said Heathcliff. 'If Cathy did not love him, I would tear his heart out and drink his blood! But while she cares about him, I will not touch a hair on his head, although I hate him.'

Isabella shouted, 'Do not speak about my brother like that!' She turned to me. 'Nellie, Heathcliff is a liar and a monster! I tried to leave him once, but I dare not try again. He only married me because I am Edgar's heir. I wish he were dead!'

Heathcliff took her arm roughly. 'Leave us! Go upstairs! I wish to speak to Nellie in private. Go!'

Heathcliff locked the door. 'Nellie, you must take a letter from me to Cathy. I must speak to her when Edgar Linton is not there. You shall not leave Wuthering Heights until you agree!'

I refused fifty times or more, but in the end I had to take the letter. I tried to give it to Cathy on the next Sunday morning when everyone else was out at church. She would not take it.

'You must read it immediately, ma'am,' I said, 'because Heathcliff is in the garden, and he is waiting for an answer.'

I heard steps on the stairs. Heathcliff had seen the unlocked door and just walked in! He walked straight to her chair, and took her in his arms and kissed her.

'Oh, Cathy!' he said when he saw how weak and ill she was.

'You and Edgar have broken my heart, Heathcliff,' she said. 'You have killed me! And how strong you are. How many years will you live after I'm gone? I want to hold you until we are both dead together!'

'You will make me as mad as yourself!' he cried.

'The master will be here soon,' I said. 'I heard him at the door.'

'I must go,' said Heathcliff.

'Do not go!' cried Cathy. 'I know this is our last time together! Edgar will not hurt you. Please stay! I shall die ...'

At that moment, Edgar walked into the room, and Cathy fell to the floor! Heathcliff picked her up in his arms, and carried her to Edgar. 'Help her first!' he said. 'You can speak to me later!'

Edgar carried Cathy to the bed. Heathcliff walked to the door. 'I shall leave this house, Nellie,' he said, 'but I shall wait in the garden!'

At about twelve o'clock that night, her daughter, also named Catherine, was born. That's the Catherine you met at Wuthering Heights, Mr Lockwood. She was a tiny seven-month-old child, because she was born two months early. Sadly her mother died two hours later, without seeing her daughter or speaking to Edgar.

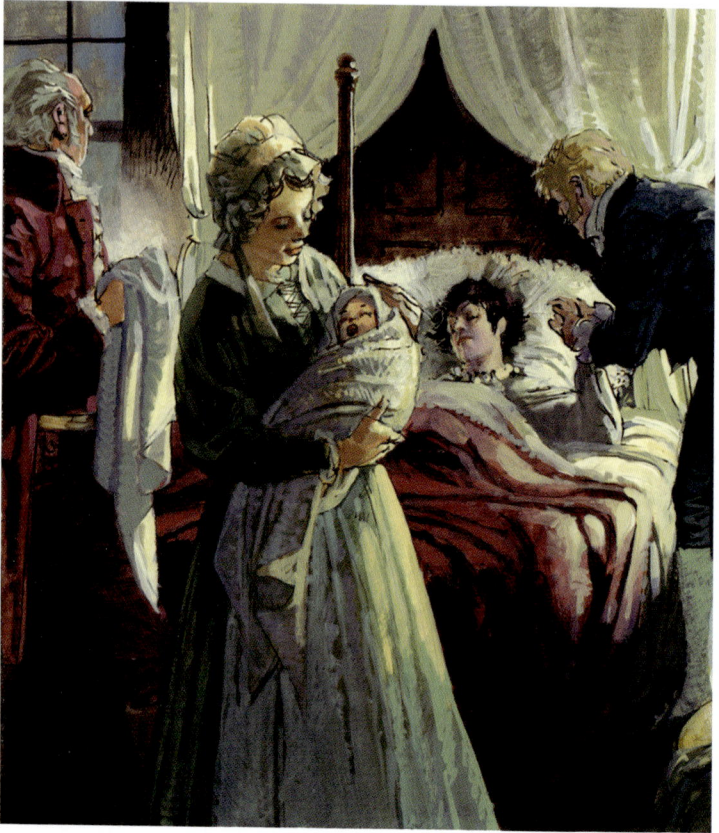

The next morning I went to the garden. Heathcliff was standing there, under an old tree.

'I know she's dead,' he said to me. 'And stop crying, Nellie. She wants none of your tears now. Tell me how she died.'

'Very quietly and peacefully,' I said. 'She never woke after you left the room yesterday.'

Heathcliff smashed his head against the tree, again and again, until blood ran down his face. Then he turned his face to the sky. 'Catherine Earnshaw!' he shouted. 'May you not rest while I am still living! You said that I killed you. Haunt me, then! I believe that ghosts walk the Earth. Haunt me always! Make me mad! But do not leave me here without you! I cannot live without you!'

Catherine's body lay in an open coffin covered with flowers. Edgar sat beside her for hours. On the second night, when I was alone in the room, I opened the window, as Heathcliff had ordered me to do. He went to the coffin, took the gold locket from her neck, and opened it. He removed the blond piece of Edgar's hair, and put a piece of his own black hair in its place, then put the locket back.

Neither her brother Hindley, nor Isabella came to her funeral. Catherine was buried in her favourite place, just outside the church graveyard, on the wild moor.

Understanding the Story 3 (Chapters 9–13)

1 **Number these events in order from 1 (earliest in the story) to 12 (latest in the story).**

_____ Heathcliff and Isabella went to live at Wuthering Heights.

_____ Heathcliff went away.

_____ Mr and Mrs Linton became sick and died.

_____ Cathy's daughter, Catherine, was born early.

_____ Edgar asked Cathy to marry him.

_____ Heathcliff returned and asked to speak to Cathy.

_____ Cathy and Edgar were married in Gimmerton.

_____ Edgar hit Heathcliff hard in the throat.

_____ Isabella ran away with Heathcliff.

_____ Cathy would not eat or drink. She was sick for many weeks.

_____ Heathcliff put a piece of his hair in Cathy's gold locket.

_____ Heathcliff heard Cathy talking to Nellie in the kitchen.

2 **Who said these things? Write their names.**

1 _____ 'I shall be the richest woman on the Yorkshire Moors.'

2 _____ 'It would degrade me to marry Heathcliff now!'

3 _____ 'I must have a few words with your mistress.'

4 _____ 'I dare not! The shock will make her mad!'

5 _____ 'If I really thought you wished me to marry Isabella, I would cut my own throat.'

6 _____ 'Your blood is ice water. And mine is hot fire!'

7 _____ 'Tell me no more about her. From this day, she is not my sister.'

8 _____ 'He only married me because I am Edgar's heir. I wish he were dead.'

9 _____ 'How many years will you live after I'm gone?'

10 _____ 'Haunt me always! Make me mad!'

3 Correct these false sentences.

1 When Heathcliff returned he was wearing the cheap clothes of a servant.

2 Heathcliff had been gone for ten years.

3 Heathcliff looked younger and shorter, and stood like a sailor.

4 Until Edgar and Cathy had a daughter, Hareton was Edgar's heir.

5 Heathcliff asked if Edgar was a man or a mouse.

6 Nellie found Isabella's little cat, hanging from a rope.

7 After six days, Isabella wrote a letter telling Edgar that she was married to Hindley.

8 Isabella said that Edgar was a liar and a monster.

9 Cathy died two days after the baby was born.

10 Hindley and Isabella came to Cathy's funeral.

14 An escape

The weather turned cold again. One night, I was sitting with the baby, Cathy, in my arms, when Isabella ran into the house. She was laughing wildly, and her thin dress was wet with rain.

'Nellie!' she said. 'Ask the servants to prepare the carriage and horses. And find me some clothes! I must go tonight. I have escaped!'

Then she took the gold wedding ring from her finger and threw it into the fire. 'There! That's the last thing I have of Heathcliff's!'

Isabella told me her story. The evening before, Heathcliff had gone out to walk on the moors. Hindley had spoken to her. 'We have both been cowards,' he had said. 'But if we work together, we can be free of him! You must sit still, and say nothing!'

Isabella continued. 'Then I saw the gun in Hindley's hand. Hindley was waiting at the door. I tried to take the gun from him, but then we heard Heathcliff returning.

I shouted that Hindley was going to murder him, and told him to go away. Heathcliff smashed the window, jumped into the room and took the gun from Hindley. Heathcliff had a knife, and cut Hindley badly. Then he threw him to the floor and started kicking him. To my surprise, he then cut off a piece of Hindley's shirt, and twisted it around his arm to stop the bleeding. "He shall not die yet," he said. "I have not finished with him."

Then he turned to me. "Get out!" he screamed. "Get out before I kill you!" He picked up a kitchen knife and threw it at my head, and it stuck in the door, just below my ear. I ran … and here I am!' she finished.

My master ordered the carriage and horses, and Isabella was driven away from the moor. She went far away to the south, near London, and there a son was born. She called him Linton, as his first name. Linton Heathcliff. She wrote that he was a weak boy, in poor health. Heathcliff heard of the child and asked for her address, but no one would give it to him.

Time passed. Edgar loved baby Cathy deeply, as I did too. She looked like her mother, except she had Edgar's blonde hair, not her mother's dark curls.

Hindley Earnshaw died at the age of twenty-seven. And Heathcliff became the master of Wuthering Heights. It was all his property. For years Hindley had lost money from his gambling. He had borrowed more and more from Heathcliff, who had always smiled to see Hindley playing cards. Heathcliff now owned the house and all the land. Young Hareton, who should have been the master of the family home, had nothing. He lived like a servant to his father's greatest enemy, except that a servant is paid. Hareton received no money and no education.

15 Two cousins

The next twelve years were the happiest time of my life, looking after Cathy. Until she was thirteen, she had never left the Linton land alone. One day, she rode off over the moor on her horse. She had always been interested in the tall rocks we could see far away across the moor. They were the rocks which her mother and Heathcliff had called their 'castle'. I went to look for her. I saw her horse outside Wuthering Heights, and hurried to the door.

Cathy was there, laughing and talking to Hareton, now a strong young man of eighteen.

'Your father will be so angry, Miss Cathy!' I said. 'Come. If you knew who owned this house, you would be happy to leave it!'

Cathy looked at Hareton. 'Isn't it your father's house?' she asked.

'No,' he grunted.

'Oh, is it your master's house? Then please go and bring me my horse. Hurry.'

'I'm not your servant,' he growled.

'He is your cousin, Hareton,' I told her. 'The son of your mother's brother, Hindley Earnshaw.'

'He is not my cousin!' she said. 'My cousin Linton lives in London, and he is a gentleman's son!'

'You have two cousins, Miss Cathy,' I told her.

It was not long after that a letter arrived, telling us that Isabella was dead. Edgar went to London to get Linton, and to bring him back to The Grange. Cathy was so excited. She had never met her cousin before, and waited for her father's carriage.

The boy looked so much like Edgar, but he was tired from the journey. I took him to his bedroom and he was soon asleep.

'Nellie, the poor boy is not strong,' said Edgar. 'But he will be a friend for Cathy. Perhaps the good air of the country and a happy house will make him healthy.'

We did not have to wait long. There was a loud knocking on the door. It was Heathcliff's servant, Joseph.

'Heathcliff has sent me for his son,' he snarled. 'And I must not go back without him.'

'Tell Mr Heathcliff his son is sleeping after his long journey,' said Edgar. 'He may go to Wuthering Heights tomorrow, but tell Mr Heathcliff that Isabella wanted him to live with me.'

'He won't care what the mother said. I must take him now.'

'You shall not have him tonight,' said Edgar.

'Then you had better bring him early tomorrow. Or Heathcliff will come himself and get him! Tell him to go away, if you dare!'

I took Linton to Wuthering Heights early the next day. The boy knew nothing of his father and asked me questions all the way. Was he a handsome man? Was he kind? Did he look like him? Why hadn't his mother and father lived together?

But what could I tell him? Not the truth, that was certain.

Heathcliff, Joseph and Hareton were waiting for us. 'Hello, Nellie. You've brought my property. Let me see it ...'

'I think Nellie's brought you a girl, by mistake,' said old Joseph.

Heathcliff laughed. 'What a pretty little thing! He's worse than I expected, Nellie. And I didn't expect much.'

I helped the frightened shaking boy from his horse.

'Stop crying!' said Heathcliff. 'That's not allowed here. Yes, you are your mother's child. I see none of me in you. Get him breakfast, Joseph. And you, Hareton, go back to your work!'

I waited until the boy was inside. 'I hope you will be kind to the boy, Heathcliff,' I said. 'Because he will not live long if you are not. Remember, he is all the family you have in the world.'

'Oh, I will be kind, Nellie. Remember, my son is the heir to The Grange and to all of Edgar Linton's property. I should not want the boy to die until I am certain that he owns it. Then of course, I will be his heir. So he will be safe with me. I have employed a teacher for him, and I've ordered Hareton to obey him. I hate the boy, just as I hated his mother, but he is mine, and one day he will be master of all the land on the moor. So, go back to your master, Nellie. Go now.'

I turned away from that cold, unhappy house. The last words I heard from the boy were 'Nellie! Do not leave me here! Nellie! I'll not stay here!'

16 Three years later

Cathy was sad that Linton had gone, and often asked about him. I met Heathcliff's new housekeeper in the village. She said the boy spent his days in his room reading. 'I've never met such a weak and whining child,' she said. 'He's ill and bad-tempered, and complains if he smells Joseph's pipe smoke, and his favourite food is warm milk.'

Cathy's sixteenth birthday was the 20th March. Her birthday was a sad, quiet day at The Grange, because it was also the date of her mother's death. Edgar always spent the day alone, and visited his wife's grave. I took Cathy walking on the moor. She loved to watch the birds out there. She could walk faster than me, and I followed her over a small hill, and stopped. By accident, we had walked onto Heathcliff's land. He was standing there with Hareton. They had not seen me.

'And who is your father?' Heathcliff was asking.

'Mr Linton of The Grange,' Cathy said. 'Is this man your son?' she pointed at Hareton.

'He is not. But you have met my son before. Hello, Nellie,' said Heathcliff as he saw me. 'You must both be tired. May I invite you to my home? You can have some tea, perhaps.'

I whispered to Cathy, 'You must certainly not go there.'

'Be quiet, Nellie,' said Heathcliff. 'Walk in front with Hareton, Cathy. You can walk with me, Nellie.' And he pulled my arm hard.

'Heathcliff, I know you have some wicked plan,' I said.

'My plan is simple,' he said. 'And I'll tell it to you honestly. I wish her to meet Linton, and for the two cousins to fall in love and get married.'

We arrived at Wuthering Heights. Linton was inside. He had grown taller. At fifteen he was a few months younger than Cathy. She greeted him with a smile and a kiss.

'Why don't you and Linton ever come to visit us?' she asked Heathcliff.

'Your father hates me,' said Heathcliff. 'He thought I was too poor to marry his sister. He will not forgive me.'

'That's so terrible! But can't Linton come on his own?'

'It's too far for me to walk,' whined Linton. 'I would be too tired.'

When we left, the three cousins stood in the door. Cathy looked up at the words cut in the stone. 'What does that say?' she asked.

'It's ... er ... writing,' said Hareton. 'I cannot read it.'

Linton laughed. 'He does not know how to read.'

Cathy looked at Hareton. 'I can't understand what he says,' she said. 'Is he stupid?'

'He's lazy and slow,' said Linton. 'He laughs at people who read books.'

'I cannot see any use for reading,' muttered Hareton angrily.

I reported everything to my master. He told Cathy she was forbidden to go there again. I hoped that was the end of it. However, a few weeks later I was cleaning Cathy's room and I found a box of letters. Cathy and Linton had been writing to each other. They were the silly love letters of children, and I made her burn them. I sent a message to Linton, saying that he would receive no more letters.

In the October, I was walking with Cathy. Heathcliff rode up and greeted us.

'I shan't speak to you,' said Cathy. 'Father says you are a wicked man, and you hate our family.'

'But I don't hate my son,' he said. 'His heart is broken. He is dying from his love for you, since your letters stopped.'

'Do not lie to the child!' I said.

'Linton dreams of you night and day,' he told Cathy. 'I am sure he is dying, and only you can save him.'

And so we went to Wuthering Heights. Linton was in a chair. 'Will you shut the door, please?' he whined. 'It's cold in here.' It did not take long for them to quarrel.

'Why do you hate my father?' he said.

'He must be cruel, that's why Aunt Isabella left him,' she said.

'She didn't leave him!' said Linton. 'But your mother hated your father, and she loved mine!'

Cathy was just like her mother. She pushed him immediately. She didn't push him hard, but he fell to the ground, coughing and crying.

We helped him get up. 'You have hurt me,' he whined. 'I shall be awake all night with this cough!'

On the way home she asked, 'What do you think of him, Nellie?'

'He's a weak, whining, complaining boy. He won't live to be twenty. I'll be surprised if he is alive next year.'

17 Cathy and Linton

The next day I was ill, and I couldn't leave my bed for three weeks. During that time, Cathy was seeing Linton regularly, every day almost. She finally told me, and I went straight to the master and told him. He ordered that the secret visits must stop.

Edgar's health was failing. He had been ill most of the year. Cathy worried about him, and did not want to make him angry. Her 17th birthday came, and for the first time Edgar did not visit his wife's grave. 'I think I will be there myself later in the year,' he said.

It was a sad time. Edgar became weaker every day. Cathy was a wonderful nurse to him. Edgar wanted her to go out and get some fresh air, so he allowed Cathy and Linton to meet once a week on the moor. I was always with her. I had told him that the boy was not like his father, and he was, of course, Edgar's nephew and the son of his dear sister.

One day, when Edgar was very ill, we had promised to meet Linton on the moor. Cathy did not want to leave her father's side, but she had promised. She thought we had to go. Linton was sitting on the ground and breathing heavily. He tried to get up when he saw us, but sat again, coughing.

'Why didn't you cancel our meeting?' she said. 'The walk has tired you, and my father is so ill.'

'I understand, but I am a coward,' he whined. 'I dare not cancel our meeting.'

'Stand up,' she said. 'And stop crying. You are degrading yourself.'

'I dare not tell you the truth, Cathy,' he said. 'But if you leave me, my father will surely kill me.'

Then I saw him, walking through the bushes towards us. Heathcliff. He called me over to him.

'Nellie!' he whispered. 'I am told that Edgar Linton is dying. Is that correct?'

'Sadly, it is true.'

'How long will he live, do you think?'

'Not long, I am sorry to say.'

'This is important. That boy must not die before his uncle.' He pointed towards the two cousins. 'Look at him, crying on the ground! Get up!' he shouted to Linton. 'Get up now!'

Heathcliff went to them. 'Catherine! Take his arm. You must help him walk back to Wuthering Heights.'

'My father has forbidden me to go there,' she replied.

Linton coughed. 'Cathy … You must come with me. Please!'

'Only as far as the door,' she said.

When we got there, Cathy went in to help Linton to his chair, and I stood outside. Suddenly Heathcliff pulled me into the house, and locked the door. 'Hareton and the servants are away,' he said. 'And you shall not leave.'

'Give me the key,' said Cathy. 'I'm not afraid of you.'

She tried to take it from his hand.

'Stop, or I will knock you down!' he shouted savagely.

She tried again and he hit her hard, on one side of the head then the other. I ran at the monster, but he knocked me to the floor.

'You cannot hit her!' I cried.

He stood over me. 'Oh, but I can. For tomorrow I shall be her father.'

He walked into the kitchen.

'What is happening, Linton?' screamed Cathy. 'Did you know this?'

He nodded. 'We are going to be married in the morning. He is afraid that I will die before your father. If we do as he wishes, we can both move to The Grange after the wedding.'

We were taken to a bedroom and locked in. At seven in the morning, Heathcliff opened the door and pulled Catherine out. I stayed a prisoner in that room for five days, before they let me out and allowed me to go downstairs.

Linton was sitting in his chair.

'Where is Cathy?' I said.

'My wife is upstairs,' he said. 'And you may not see her. You can go to The Grange now. Remember, it will all be mine when my uncle dies! '

I hurried across the moor, thinking I must get help to rescue her. I found a sad sight, as poor Edgar was close to his end. He sent a man to bring a lawyer so that he could change his heir, and he sent four men to get Cathy. They returned without her. Heathcliff said she was ill and would not let them in. The lawyer was not at home.

I decided to take the men servants with guns, and to go and get Cathy myself the next day. But at three o'clock in the morning there was a knock on the door. It was Cathy.

'Is he still alive?' she called.

'Yes, but it will not be long,' I said. 'Cathy, I will ask you to lie. Tell him that you are happy with Linton. Let him die in peace.'

18 The new master

The lawyer, Mr Green, was at The Grange the same evening. We discovered why he had not been 'at home'. He was working for Heathcliff. He told all the servants, except me, that they must find new jobs. He said that he was working for Linton Heathcliff, the new owner of The Grange and all Edgar's property.

I found that Linton had unlocked the door for Cathy and let her out. He was nearly as afraid of her as he was of his father.

Heathcliff arrived at The Grange after the funeral to get Cathy. 'Get your things,' he said. 'I want my family around me.'

She looked at him. 'Nobody loves you,' she said. 'Nobody will cry when you die. I would not be you!'

I asked to go to Wuthering Heights with her, but Heathcliff told me to stay at The Grange as housekeeper. He did not want Cathy to have a friend.

Linton did not live many weeks. Cathy was a good nurse to him too, but Heathcliff never visited his son. As soon as he was dead, Heathcliff and the lawyer explained that all Linton's property now belonged to his father. Heathcliff was the master, and Cathy had no money, no property and no friends.

Mr Lockwood's story

Mrs Dean's story ended there. I had to go back to London and I never expected to see those moors again. But I visited the area on business six months later in September 1802, and decided to go and see Mrs Dean. I asked at The Grange, but the new housekeeper told me that Nellie Dean was now at Wuthering Heights.

I rode to the house and walked to the door. The window was open. I heard soft voices.

'Cloud, you fool, C-L-O-U-D. Now remember that or I shall pull your hair!'

'Cloud. Now kiss me, because I remembered it.'

'First read to me again, with no mistakes, and then I might kiss you.'

It was Cathy and Harcton. I went quietly round to the kitchen door. Mrs Dean was working there. She was pleased to see me and invited me in. I asked if Mr Heathcliff was at home.

'Have you not heard about Heathcliff's death?' she said. 'It was three months ago. Sit there, and I'll tell you the story ...'

Nellie Dean's story

After you left The Grange, sir, I moved back to Wuthering Heights. I was happy to be near Cathy again. After a time, she and Hareton became friends. She would joke with him because he could not read, and finally she agreed to teach him. One day she asked Hareton to take out some old bushes, so she could grow flowers. Heathcliff was angry.

'What are you doing to my land?' he shouted.

'Well, you have stolen all my land and all my money,' she said.

'Be quiet, or I'll knock you down!'

'If you try, Hareton will knock you down first!'

I expected a fight, but Heathcliff stopped. 'You must try not to make me angry,' he said. 'Or I really shall murder you both one day.'

I was surprised. After that, Heathcliff changed. He did not eat with us, and often he walked across the moors all night. He said strange things. One night I took his dinner to him. He was in his room. He looked at me, and whispered, 'Nellie ... Are we alone? Are we by ourselves?'

'Yes, sir.'

'I think we are not,' he muttered.

'Do you feel ill?' I asked.

'No, and I am not afraid of death. I have to tell myself to breathe. I have to remind my heart to beat. I wish it would all end.'

When I left the room, I heard his voice. 'Catherine! Oh, Catherine! Are you there?'

The next night he did not go to his room as usual. We heard him go upstairs to Catherine Earnshaw's old room. I went up in the morning with his breakfast. The window was open, and he was lying on the bed. His eyes were wide open. He seemed to be smiling. He was dead.

We buried him next to Catherine on the moor.

But there is a happy ending. Cathy and Hareton are getting married on New Year's Day, and then we shall all move to The Grange. They will sell this unhappy house.

Mr Lockwood

I walked across the moors slowly and stopped to look at the three graves. Catherine's was the middle one, grey, almost twenty years old. Edgar's had grass already growing on it. Heathcliff's was new. I hoped that any ghosts were now quiet and at rest.

The End

Understanding the Story 4
(Chapters 14–18)

1 **Number these events in order from 1 (earliest in the story) to 12 (latest in the story).**

_____ Linton was born near London, in the south.

_____ When Cathy first met Hareton on the moor, she was thirteen.

_____ Heathcliff made Linton and Cathy get married.

_____ Hindley tried to murder Heathcliff.

_____ Heathcliff took Linton to live with him.

_____ Edgar died before he could change his will.

_____ Heathcliff died in Catherine's old room.

_____ Isabella escaped from Wuthering Heights and went to the south.

_____ Cathy started meeting Linton regularly.

_____ Linton was sent to Yorkshire after his mother died.

_____ Linton died and Heathcliff owned The Grange too.

_____ Hindley died, and Heathcliff became the owner of Wuthering Heights.

2 **Who said these things? Write their names.**

1 _____ 'Find me some clothes. I must go tonight. I have escaped!'

2 _____ 'He shall not die yet. I have not finished with him.'

3 _____ 'Heathcliff has sent me for his son. And I must not go back without him.'

4 _____ 'He's worse than I expected, Nellie. And I didn't expect much.'

5 _____ 'Your mother hated your father, and she loved mine!'

6 _____ 'My father has forbidden me to go there.'

7 _____ 'Remember, that it will all be mine when my uncle dies.'

8 _____ 'Nobody will cry when you die. I would not be you!'

9 _____ 'Now kiss me, because I remembered it.'

10 _____ 'I am not afraid of death. I have to tell myself to breathe.'

3 Are these sentences true (✓) or false (✗)? Correct the false ones.

1 ☐ After Hindley died, Hareton received no money and no education.

2 ☐ Heathcliff went to London to get Linton.

3 ☐ Heathcliff employed a teacher for Hareton.

4 ☐ Cathy's birthday was the same date as her mother's death.

5 ☐ Nellie found a box of love letters from Hareton.

6 ☐ Nellie was a prisoner at Wuthering Heights for ten days.

7 ☐ Edgar's lawyer was really working for Heathcliff.

8 ☐ Linton got all Edgar's money, then died.

The language of Wuthering Heights

shall
In 1848 *shall/shan't* was used with *I* and *we* much more than it is in modern English. Many examples of *shall* in the story would be *will* or *'ll* nowadays. *Shall* is not wrong, but it sounds formal. People used to be more formal.

When *shall* is used with the second or third person, e.g., *You shall do it!* it is a strong obligation, like *must.* Similarly, *will* with the first person was stronger than *shall* in 1848. *I will do it! You shall not stop me!*

Contractions
Contractions like *don't, won't* and *hasn't* were less frequently used in speech, certainly among educated people.

Names
Mrs is a short form which comes from *mistress* and *Mr* comes from *master*. Because Nellie is a servant she talks about the *master* and *mistress* of the house: her employers – *Mr and Mrs Earnshaw.*

Nellie says *Miss Cathy* or *Miss* to Catherine until she is married. Then she says *ma'am* (madam) or *Mrs Linton*.

Nellie also talks about *Mr Edgar* and *Miss Cathy*. We do not use *Mr/Miss* with first names in modern English any more, but it is what a servant would say when talking about a child of the house – the father is *Mr Linton*, the son is *Mr Edgar*, the mother is *Mrs Linton*, the daughter is *Miss Isabella*.

Glossary

These words are not in the 1,500 vocabulary words for Level 5.

affectionate loving, but not romantic love. We can feel affectionate to children, friends, animals, family as well as husbands or wives

ankle the part joining the foot to the leg

candle a candle is round, made of wax, with a string in the middle; you burn it to give light

carriage you ride in a carriage; it has wheels and is pulled by horses (also in modern English 'railway carriage')

coffin dead people are buried in a wooden coffin

coward someone who is afraid, usually afraid to fight

curly, curls when hair is not straight, but has bends in it

degrade make lower, make worse

enquire to ask about something

furniture the things in a house: chairs, tables, sofas, cupboards

gamble to play cards, or roulette, or put money on a horse race, or any sports contest. Gamblers hope to win money

grave when people die, they are buried in a grave

graveyard an area with graves (more often 'cemetery' in modern English)

gypsy a person who speaks the Romany language. A gypsy lives in many different countries and travels around from place to place. In modern English, the polite word is 'traveller'

haunt we say that ghosts haunt living people. A building where people say they have seen ghosts is a haunted building

heir your heir is the person who gets your land and money when you die. In England, in 1848, when the book was written, the laws about heirs were very different, and they were also different from family to family. In this story, a male heir comes first in each generation. So Linton, not Cathy, is the heir

housekeeper a person, usually a woman, who looks after a house as a job; often 'chief female servant' in a large house

lamb a young sheep

landlord someone who rents out a house or a room for money

late 'the late Mrs Linton' tells us that Mrs Linton is dead

locket a piece of jewellery. It is worn around the neck on a chain, and is a small metal box in which you can put a picture

moor(s) wild, open country; moors have few or no trees

pay someone back to take revenge on someone

pinch to take someone's skin between two fingers and press so that it hurts

property something you own is your property

rags old clothes which are torn

revenge when someone has hurt you or done something wrong to you, revenge is the way you punish them

roughly in a violent way; not softly or gently

soul the part of someone that is believed to continue after the person is dead

stable a building where horses live

throat the front part of the neck

whine, whining to speak in a high, complaining voice

widow a woman whose husband has died

Yorkshire an area in the north-east of England: Leeds, Sheffield, York and Hull are important cities in Yorkshire

Activities

1 Look at the story again and find this information. How fast can you find it?

1 What was the date cut in the stone over the door at Wuthering Heights?

2 Where did Mr Earnshaw first find Heathcliff?

3 What did Heathcliff pour on Edgar's head?

4 What was Hareton's mother's name?

5 What was the month and year when Hareton was born?

6 What was the date when Catherine Linton died?

7 What colour was Isabella's small dog?

8 What was the name of the nearest village to the houses?

9 Young Cathy was born early. How early?

10 What was in Catherine Linton's locket when she was buried?

11 Where was Linton born?

12 How old was Hindley at the time of his death?

2   Are these sentences (✓) or false (✗)? Correct the false ones.

1   ☐ Mr Lockwood was attacked by three dogs.

2   ☐ The Grange was three miles from Wuthering Heights.

3   ☐ Old Mr Earnshaw bought three horses for the children.

4   ☐ After the fight between Edgar and Heathcliff, Catherine stayed in her room for three days and three nights.

5   ☐ Catherine died three hours after her daughter was born.

6   ☐ Young Cathy had three cousins.

7   ☐ Hareton was three years older than young Cathy.

8   ☐ Nellie could not leave her bed for three months.

9   ☐ Nellie was a prisoner for three days.

10 ☐ Mr Lockwood stopped to look at the three graves.

3   Complete the sentences with words from the glossary.

1   Her husband died ten years ago, so she has been a _____ for ten years.

2   These socks feel too small around my _____.

3   I think I've got flu. When I speak, my _____ hurts.

4   The field was full of sheep, with baby _____.

5   The shop sold _____. There were some nice chairs and tables in the shop window.

6   At the funeral, they put the _____ into the grave.

7 The electric lights went out, so we had to light some
_____.

8 He used to _____ on card games and he lost all his
money.

9 She got home and put the horse in its _____.

10 His clothes were very old and full of holes. They were
_____.

11 She had a silver _____ around her neck with a
photo of her parents inside.

12 He won't fight! He's afraid. He's a _____.

13 She has straight hair, but her sister has _____ hair.

14 The _____ arrived to collect the rent for the house.

15 I lost my phone on the train. I went to the lost
_____ office, but they didn't have it.

16 Leeds is the largest city in _____.

17 In old stories, ghosts sometimes _____ graveyards.

18 'Stop _____! There's nothing wrong with you,' said
the little boy's mother.

19 The other team beat us because they cheated. We will
have our _____ next time we play!

20 It's a very nice dog. It's friendly and _____ towards
everyone, especially children.

4 <u>Underline</u> the correct family word in each sentence.

1 Hareton was Hindley's (*son / nephew*).

2 Young Cathy was Heathcliff's (*daughter / daughter-in-law*).

3 Linton was Edgar's (*son-in-law / son*).

4 Young Cathy was Isabella's (*niece / cousin*).

5 Hareton and young Cathy were (*cousins / brother and sister*).

6 Edgar was young Cathy's (*brother / father*).

7 Frances was Hindley's (*wife / sister*).

8 Heathcliff was Linton's (*father / uncle*).

9 Isabella was young Cathy's (*mother / aunt*).

10 Young Cathy was Edgar's (*daughter / niece*).

5 Discuss these questions.

1 Was Mr Lockwood a welcome guest? How did they greet him?

2 Describe the place where Mr Lockwood slept at Wuthering Heights.

3 What did Mr Lockwood see? Do you think it was only a dream?

4 Why was Heathcliff talking about the candle by the window? What did he think it would do?

5 Why did Hindley bully Heathcliff?

6 Describe Cathy and Heathcliff's first visit to The Grange. What happened?

7   How had Cathy changed while she was staying with Edgar and Isabella?

8   Why did Heathcliff leave Wuthering Heights? How long was he away?

9   We don't know what he was doing while he was away. Can you guess? How did he become rich? (The answer is not in the story. Imagine.)

10   What happened when Heathcliff returned?

11   Describe the fight between Edgar and Heathcliff. What happened?

12   Why did Heathcliff pretend to like Isabella?

13   How did Catherine die? Do you think she was 'mad'?

14   Why couldn't Linton stay at The Grange with Edgar?

15   What was Heathcliff's main reason for wanting Linton to live with him?

16   What happened to Hindley's money? Who had loaned him money?

17   Did Linton really love young Cathy?

18   Was Hareton really 'lazy and slow'?

19   Did Heathcliff want to die? Why?

20   What is the 'happy ending'?